THE ROYAL BORDER BRIDGE

Carrying the East coast main line from England into Scotland

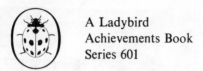

A Ladybird
Achievements Book
Series 601

Here is the fascinating story of railways in Britain—from the earliest pioneer days of 'Puffing Billy' and the 'Rocket' to 'Mallard' and the latest diesel and electric locomotives.

Magnificently illustrated by Robert Ayton, this is a book for everyone who loves trains.

A Ladybird 'Achievements' Book

THE STORY OF
RAILWAYS

by RICHARD BOWOOD
with illustrations by ROBERT AYTON

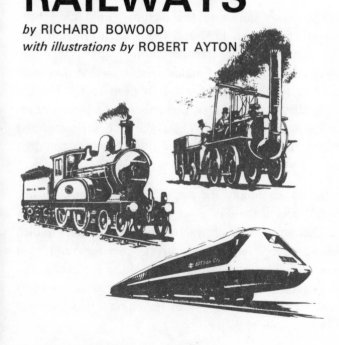

Ladybird Books Loughborough

The First Railways

The picture shows the first kind of railway, used at coal mines to haul coal from the pithead. This was before locomotives—steam engines which drive themselves—had been invented. The advantage of the railway was that when wheels could run on smooth plates, or on iron rails, they were much easier to haul. The trucks were pulled by horses, or sometimes by a rope connected to a stationary steam engine.

The scene shown in the picture would have been sometime between 1790 and 1820, when Great Britain led the world in transportation. John McAdam invented a new way of making roads so that they were hard enough not to be cut into deep ruts. Thomas Telford, the poet son of a shepherd, made fine roads and wonderful bridges. The Duke of Bridgewater and others constructed canals along which goods could be carried by barges.

It was essentially the age of the horse, and no one could foresee the day when the horse would no longer be the only form of tractive power. Horses pulled drays, wagons and carts, private carriages and mail coaches. They pulled the barges along the canals and they hauled the trucks on the mine railways. Horseback was the normal way of travelling. 'Horsepower' was then—*horse power*.

An early colliery railway

The Surrey Iron Railway

The first public railway in the world came into being as a result of Britain's war with the France of Napoleon. It was the custom to carry goods from ships at Portsmouth to London by coastal vessels, but there was always the danger that the French fleet might sail into the Channel. So a horse-tramway was begun to link London and Portsmouth.

The danger was removed in 1805 when Lord Nelson defeated the combined fleets of France and Spain at Trafalgar, and the new railway was not continued beyond Merstham, nineteen miles south of London. Nevertheless this was a public railway, with trucks drawn by horses. It was used mainly to carry coal, bricks, lime and sand, and it was never meant to carry passengers.

It was not a proper railway, of course; no passengers were carried and it did not run to a timetable. There were no stations. More horse-drawn railways were built in other parts of the country for carrying heavy goods. A flat truck was attached, on which the horse could ride when the train was running down a gradient. The Surrey Iron Railway was considered a wonderful idea at the time, and no one could have foreseen the day when railway lines would be laid throughout the land.

PRIVATE
SURREY
IRON
RAILWAY

The First Steam Engine

Railways as we know them were born of the steam engine, and the name we honour as the first inventor is a Cornishman, Richard Trevithick.

Trevithick was a very strong man, and he was quick with figures. He also had a most inventive mind. He was the engineer of a tin mine near Penzance, and in 1797 when he set about improving the rather wheezy stationary engine, he had a great idea. Would it not be possible, he thought, to make a steam engine on wheels, which would use its own power to drive itself along? A kind of iron horse?

In 1804 he made his first steam engine, the first in the world. It ran on iron wheels on rails at the Pen-y-Darren mineral railroad in Wales. The next one he made was put to work at a Tyneside colliery.

But Trevithick was twenty years in advance of the times; no one really saw the possibilities in the strange and fearsome looking engines. He tried to prove their value by running a passenger train, hauled by a steam engine, round a small circular track on some waste ground in London. People paid for the ride, but saw it only as a fair-ground novelty.

'Puffing Billy'

The scene of the next important event in our story is a four mile stretch of line at the Wylam Colliery, near Newcastle-upon-Tyne. It was one of the oldest horse-tramways in the country, where horses hauled wagons of coal from the pithead to the River Tyne. There the coal was loaded into barges whicn took it down the river to Newcastle, to be shipped to London.

It was on this short stretch of line that a very famous locomotive made its first run. It was built in 1813 by William Hedley, of the Wylam Colliery, with the help of the principal engineer and the foreman blacksmith. The engine was so noisy, and emitted so much smoke that it was called 'Puffing Billy.'

'Puffing Billy' started to work for the colliery in 1814. She was modified and improved, and for a time she was put on eight wheels instead of four. She was not fast, nor handsome, but she was so efficient that she hauled coal trucks for the colliery for nearly fifty years.

She retired in 1862 and was sent to the Patents' Museum in London, a forerunner of the Science Museum. You can still see 'Puffing Billy' in a well-deserved place of honour in the Science Museum.

George Stephenson

George Stephenson was born in 1781, the son of the stoker of a colliery engine at Wylam, where 'Puffing Billy' was later to run. When he was fourteen George went to work, for a shilling a day, as his father's assistant. He learnt to read and write in his spare time, and studied everything to do with steam engines, which were his passion.

In those days a number of engineers were trying to design and build efficient steam locomotives, and none of them was more enthusiastic or painstaking than George Stephenson. He and his son Robert were destined to become the greatest names in the story of railways.

George Stephenson built his first engine in 1814, and a more successful one the next year. He was also an expert in railway construction. When a new public railway was constructed between Stockton and Darlington, George Stephenson was the surveyor and engineer. The railway was opened in 1825, and the first train was hauled by a new engine, built by George Stephenson, called 'Locomotion.'

'Locomotion' created a sensation, for it achieved a speed of twenty miles an hour. It also had the distinction of hauling the first train on the first *public* railway in the world with a steam locomotive.

The Liverpool and Manchester Railway

The Stockton and Darlington Railway was originally intended for goods traffic only. The first complete railway for passenger and goods traffic, with trains running to a timetable, was the Liverpool and Manchester Railway which opened in 1830.

Bitter opposition had to be overcome in Parliament before the line could be built. Landowners objected to the line crossing and spoiling their land, farmers said their cows would go dry at the sight of a steam engine, and many people dreaded terrible accidents.

Permission was at last obtained and George Stephenson was appointed Chief Engineer of the new railway. The thirty-five miles of line was built between Liverpool and Manchester, and many engineering problems had to be solved.

The main difficulties were making the tunnels at the Liverpool end of the line, and building an embankment across the wide stretch of marshland known as Chat Moss. It seemed for a time that the embankment would never be built; everything they put in to provide foundations just sank into the marsh. But Stephenson had the patience which goes with genius. He persevered, and by 1830 the new line was completed.

'The Rocket'

When the Liverpool and Manchester Railway was nearing completion, the Directors announced a competition with a prize of £500 for the most efficient railway engine. Tests were held at Rainhill, near Liverpool, and the engines were expected to be able to run at eight to ten miles an hour.

Five different engines were entered for the competition, but there was no doubt about the winner. It was 'The Rocket,' designed and driven by George Stephenson, and built by his son Robert. This famous engine passed every test in the competition and travelled at the unheard-of speed of twenty-nine miles per hour.

Thus it was that when the line was formally opened in 1830, George Stephenson, who had supervised the construction of the line, drove the first engine. This was 'The Northumbrian,' designed very like 'The Rocket' herself, which hauled the fourth train in a triumphal procession that marked the historic occasion. There was a large crowd, with the Duke of Wellington as the Guest of Honour.

With the opening of the first passenger railway in the world a new age, *The Railway Age*, had dawned.

'The Planet-Patentee'

Boys who watched 'The Rocket' puffing along at nearly thirty miles an hour would have gazed with the same awe and wonder as a modern boy has for a supersonic jet aeroplane in flight. 'The Rocket' was, however, more the final version of the experimental engines than the forerunner of the ones to come.

'The Rocket' had single driving wheels leading, a single carrying axle supporting the firebox, and inclined external cylinders at the rear. Within a few months of 'The Rocket's' appearance an even better locomotive was tested and proved, the engine which pointed the way to the engines of the future.

This was 'The Planet,' built by George Stephenson's son Robert and tested at the end of 1830. It was the first engine to combine horizontal cylinders encased under the smokebox in front, a cranked axle and a multitubular boiler. In its final version 'The Planet' had six wheels, arranged 2-2-2, for passenger locomotives.

'The Planet' was, in fact, an elementary form of the later locomotives, and it proved itself by giving highly efficient service.

'The Planet-Patentee' of the 1830's

The Revolution Caused by the Railway

When the stationary steam engine became available to provide works and factories with the new source of power, a great change began in Britain's way of life. Where coal was easily obtained new factories sprang up, and around them new towns, usually of hideous little houses. Industry increased a hundredfold, and the 'industrial revolution' brought about a new England; there was abundant employment, ugliness, and great wealth.

The roads could not carry away the ever-increasing quantities of goods the factories produced, nor could the canals. The railway with the steam locomotive came just when it was urgently needed. Far-seeing men began to plan railways up and down the country, linking the cities and the ports.

The new railway system was to be like the arteries in a body, along which the products of industry could flow, from the factories to the markets, and to the ports. From the ports the goods could be shipped abroad, and from those exports would come the wealth to make Great Britain the richest country in the world.

So the surveyors, the civil engineers, and the labourers (the 'navvies' as they were called), were busy as beavers and the shining rails spread up and down, and across the land.

Making a tunnel for a new railway

'Railway Fever'

Only eight years after the Liverpool and Manchester Railway was opened there were more than 1800 miles of railway line in operation in Britain, and a number of different companies. Think of the work the building of a railway line entails; the cuttings and embankments to avoid steep gradients, the tunnels and bridges, the stations and sidings, and the locomotives and rolling stock. It was all pioneer work and it could only have been done by a country which was in a fever—the 'Railway Fever.'

Enough skilled engineers had to be found; also the surveyors and labour. The number of trains in service was constantly increasing, and locomotives were improved, so that by 1848 the journey of 393 miles between London and Edinburgh, was made regularly in 13 hours.

Railway travel was not very comfortable in those days. The first-class passengers were well enough in sprung and padded coaches, but the second-class travelled in box-like affairs, and the third class sat on wooden benches in open trucks.

Britain had, with justice, been proud of her stage coach system, but the gaily painted and lovely coaches which had sped along the roads behind their fine horses were no longer required. They were sold cheap, and often became chicken houses.

A station scene in the early days

The Royal Mail

The Grand Junction Railway was opened in 1837, from Birmingham to Newton Junction, thus connecting with the Liverpool and Manchester Railway. On the first day of the new railway an important experiment was made. The General Post Office in London sent mail bags to Birmingham in the usual way, by mail coach. At Birmingham the mail was loaded into the first train to leave on the new railway. The next day the letters were delivered in Manchester and Liverpool.

Soon a horse-box was added to the train and converted to be used as a letter-sorting carriage. A device was added for picking up mail bags without the train stopping. Then special coaches were built and attached to trains as travelling post offices. As the railways spread over the whole country, the mail went by train, and letters were delivered much more quickly.

Thus a third important use was found for the railways; first they carried goods, then passengers, and finally the mail. Once it was the mail coaches, now it was the railways. As the idea developed, special mail trains were put into service, with the sorters working in their travelling post offices as the trains ran through the night.

The First Royal Train

June 13th, 1842, was a great day for railways, for suddenly railway travel became respectable. Until then middle-class people were very doubtful. You had to travel with all sorts of people and sit with strangers. It also seemed a very dangerous thing to do, because trains travelled at thirty miles an hour and more. It was much safer and more respectable to go in your own carriage and a pair of horses.

However on that June 13th all such doubts were banished for good, for Queen Victoria herself travelled in a train. The royal party drove to Slough station, where Her Majesty inspected the line, the engine and the special saloon built for the occasion. At noon exactly the royal train left for Paddington. The engine was driven by the Superintendent of the railway company's locomotive department, and with him on the footplate was the famous engineer, I. K. Brunel.

At 12.25 the train drew into Paddington, where many officials and a large crowd waited anxiously, There was an escort of Hussars, a red carpet and handsome decorations. To everyone's relief it was learned that Her Majesty had enjoyed the journey and expressed herself quite charmed with it. From that moment there was no doubt at all about the safety, or the respectability, of railway travel.

Saloon of Queen Victoria's train

The Battle of the Gauges

The first railway companies planned their relatively short lengths of railway in a haphazard way about the country. Gradually, however, larger systems emerged, joining up several small companies, until there were three large railway companies, as well as many small ones. The large companies were the London and North Western Railway, the Great Western, from London to Bristol (which had the great I. K. Brunel as its chief engineer), and the South Western Railway from London to Southampton.

There was great rivalry between the three companies: in locomotive design, in speed, in comfort and in fares. But there was a much more important question to be solved, 'the battle of the gauges.'

Brunel believed that greater safety and comfort was obtained with wider rails than the other railways used, and the Great Western built its line with the rails seven feet and a quarter-inch apart—the broad gauge. The other lines were built with the rails four feet, eight-and-a-half-inches apart. If trains were to run from one system to another, something had to be done. Which should change? The long and bitter battle was ended when Parliament passed the Gauge Act, making it unlawful to build a railway of more than four feet, eight-and-a-half-inch gauge.

A dual gauge track

Branch Lines

When the main lines had been built up and down the country the branch lines came into being, slender tentacles stretching out to remoter parts. Some country towns resolutely refused to have a railway, trying to hold on to the older and quieter days which were swiftly passing. When they came to see what they had missed they had to be content with a very minor branch line, so they remained small and unimportant while their more far-sighted neighbours prospered by being connected to the main system.

It seemed likely that the horse population of the country would dwindle with the growth of the railway, but the effect was the opposite. Horses were in demand more than before, for cabs, for the station bus and for the heavy drays which took goods to and from the stations.

In the past, country people had often spent their whole lives without ever going further than ten miles from their village. The railway changed that; it was possible to get to a branch line station and then to travel quickly to town or city, to London or to the seaside for holidays. As well as the busy main line stations, the friendly little country stations came into being.

A country station in 1870

The Forth Bridge

When you travel by train, do you ever think of the engineering feat entailed in the building of the line? We usually take it all for granted; the track cutting its way across the countryside, with its carefully calculated curves, embankments and cuttings, tunnels and bridges.

Perhaps the most momentous engineering feat of all was the building of the Forth Bridge to cross the Firth of Forth, north-west of Edinburgh. Faith in such ambitious bridges had been tragically shaken by the Tay Bridge disaster. This great bridge across the Firth of Tay was the pride of the country. But its construction was faulty and one winter's night in 1879, when a strong westerly gale was blowing, the bridge broke. A train crossing it was hurled into the waters below. There were no survivors.

Nevertheless a new Tay Bridge was built, and in 1890, the Prince of Wales opened an even greater one, the Forth Bridge. At the time it was the longest bridge in the world, with three cantilever towers three hundred and thirty feet high, and a span of one thousand, seven hundred and ten feet. The Forth Bridge has been in use ever since. It is an awe-inspiring sight with its delicate tracery of steel spanning the waters of the Firth of Forth.

'The Golden Age'

The period from about 1890 to 1914 can be called 'The Golden Age' of the railways. Lines were established all over the British Isles: the great trunk lines, main lines and branch lines, so that few people were very far from a railway. Locomotives, rolling stock, administration and organization had reached a high peak of efficiency. The motor car was only a novelty, so the railways had the monopoly of long distance travel.

Railwaymen and their regular passengers had a great pride in their own line. They were convinced that *their* line was the best. Locomotives and carriages were painted in bright colours, and they were lovingly polished and cleaned. They were proud days.

The big Companies had their crack trains on long runs, and the drivers of the giant locomotives which hauled them took punctuality as a matter of personal honour. The most famous of these trains was 'The Flying Scotsman.' Since 1862 this train has left King's Cross every day at ten o'clock in the morning for Edinburgh, except for a few days during the two world wars, when the line was closed through enemy action.

'*The Flying Scotsman*' *in* 1907

Boat-Trains

When the passengers take their seats in an Ocean Boat-Train at the London terminus, hear the doors slam and the whistle blow, they say their last farewells to their friends. As the train pulls out of the station their journey across the world has begun. The boat-trains are special ones, running to connect with the liners at the ports—Tilbury, Southampton, Liverpool or Glasgow. They run on to the quayside, so that it is only a few steps from the train to the gangway of the ship.

There are other boat-trains, too, which have run regularly since the early days of the railways, to connect with ships for the Continent, the Channel Islands and Ireland. These trains also run on to the quays beside the ships. Some continental boat-trains run on to the ship, the train-ferry, and cross the Channel to continue on the other side.

It is the boat-trains which bring people returning home from abroad, and foreign visitors, who get from them their first view of the English countryside. It is also from these trains that the visitor gets his first idea of the way we manage things in Britain. Fortunately we can be proud of our railways.

The Underground Railway

Great Britain has led the world in nearly every aspect of railway development, and the worlds' first city underground line was opened in London as long ago as 1863. It was the beginning of our Metropolitan Line, which joined Paddington and Farringdon Street. It was not properly an underground railway; it was a covered way which did not go to any depth. In 1868 the District Railway was opened, running between South Kensington and Westminster.

The locomotives were supposed to work in the tunnels without emitting smoke or steam, but in fact the air became so foul that ventilating openings had to be made. The carriages were dimly lit and stuffy, but the 'Met' and the 'District' were very popular and were rapidly extended.

The first deep-level electric railway, or 'tube,' was opened in London in 1890—The City and South London Railway. It ran from King William Street in the City to Stockwell, and proved to be an immediate success. From that beginning has grown the elaborate network of underground railways in London, at a depth from twenty to one hundred and ninety feet. The brightly lit stations, the escalators, and the smooth-running trains with their automatic doors carry millions of Londoners to and from their work every day.

'British Railways'

During the First World War the railways were worked at great pressure with only the minimum of maintenance and no renewal. When the war ended in 1918 it was found that drastic measures would have to be taken to restore them to efficiency again.

Moreover, the motor car, the lorry and the motor coach had come on the scene, and the railways no longer had the monopoly of transport.

It was decided that the way to effect the necessary economies and to increase efficiency was to merge the many companies into four Group Companies. It was done by Act of Parliament, and on January 1st, 1923, one hundred and twenty-three separate companies were amalgamated to form 'The Big Four.' These were the Great Western, the London, Midland and Scottish, the London and North Eastern and the Southern Railways.

During the Second World War the railways were again controlled by the Government. Because of the tremendous war effort they were desperately overworked. When the war was won the railways were in dire need of help and this time an even more drastic step was taken. On January 1st, 1948, the railways were nationalized, that is they were taken over completely by the Government. In place of the four group names there is now but one—'British Railways', the responsibility resting with the British Railways Board.

Building a new locomotive

The Signal Box

As we sit in a train speeding along the smooth rails, how often do we think of the signalmen who are watching our train and passing it on from stretch to stretch of line? Not very often perhaps, yet on these men, and the signalling system, depends the safety of railway travel.

Soon after the Liverpool and Manchester Railway was opened in 1830 fixed signals were set up, and in 1841 the familiar semaphore type was introduced. The electric telegraph, linking the signal boxes along the route, was first used in 1837, and the next step was the 'block system', by which the line is divided into sections, and only when the next one is clear is a train passed on to it.

The signalling system has been improved from time to time; automatic colour light signals were first used in 1928, and now more advanced types of colour light signals and the automatic warning system have been installed.

The modern signal box at Newcastle-upon-Tyne Central station does the work of four old-type signal boxes. It is all-electric and controls ten miles of track, including the approaches to the station where, in the morning peak period, 51 trains leave within 60 minutes.

A modern signal box

Coaches and Carriages

The early railway travellers could never have dreamed of the comfort we take for granted. For a long time only the first-class compartments were upholstered, and when the third-class passenger was promoted from open trucks to a closed carriage he had but little comfort. Not even the first-class carriages were heated, the only lighting was from smelly oil lamps, and there were, of course, no corridors.

Step by step the improvements were made, as each company tried to do better than the others. Gas lighting was introduced first, and then electric. Footwarmers were provided, which the passenger could fill with hot water, and later steam was conducted through the train from the engine. In 1892 the first corridor train came into service.

Gradually comfort became general for all three classes and third-class compartments were upholstered and carpeted. The second-class went out of service, and eventually the thirds were classified as second-class. Other improvements were dining-cars and buffet-cars and, for long night runs, sleeping-cars.

A modern first-class compartment

Giant Steam Locomotives

Boys, and their fathers too, have always admired and loved railway engines. There was majesty in the suppressed power of a steam locomotive, shining and hissing as she stood ready to haul her long train along the shining rails. Train enthusiasts knew by heart the aristocrats, and there was an unbroken succession of them since Stephenson's 'Rocket' first ran.

The last word in express steam engines was the British Railways standard locomotive No. 71,000, named 'The Duke of Gloucester'. She was a Pacific type, 4-6-2, fitted with British Caprotti poppet valve gear. Roller bearing axle-boxes were fitted throughout. 'The Rocket' weighed 4 tons; 'The Duke of Gloucester' weighed 156 tons. To see her hauling the 'Mid-day Scot' from Euston to Glasgow was always an awe-inspiring sight indeed.

The picture on the opposite page shows a world-famous locomotive. She was another Pacific class, No. 60022, and named 'Mallard'. She held the world's speed record for steam traction. Hauling a test train between Grantham and Peterborough on July 3rd, 1938, she attained a speed of one hundred and twenty-six m.p.h.

'Mallard'— the world's fastest steam locomotive

Diesel and Electric Locomotives

Britain invented the steam engine and the country is rich in coal, so it is sad to think that the last steam locomotive to be built for Britain's railways left the workshops in 1960. But a great national railway system cannot be run on sentiment and the steam engine, therefore, has had to give way to the greater efficiency and economy of diesel and electric power.

Apart from being cleaner and ready for service at the push of a button, diesel and electric powered locomotives and trains are able to accelerate faster, pull heavier loads and run at higher speeds than the steam engine.

Of these two forms of power, diesel is a comparative newcomer, for electric trains began to run in Britain as long ago as 1904 between Newcastle-on-Tyne and Benton. Today electrification is widespread and covers most of the lines between London and the South Coast and London to Southend, Chelmsford and Bishops Stortford, lines in and around Glasgow, and the busy main routes between London and the Midlands and between Liverpool and Manchester. Plans are also in hand for further electrification of other main-line and suburban services.

Diesel power came into use on Britain's main lines in the 1960's, although a large number of diesel shunters were in service well before that time and the Great Western Railway had a few diesel railcars in service in the 1930's. Today diesel power is used to haul all services on non-electrified routes, including such famous expresses as the Flying Scotsman and the Cornish Riviera Express.

48

A diesel locomotive (above) and an electric locomotive (below)

More Speed

Diesel and electric power have enabled train speeds to be increased dramatically over the past few years and today many expresses run at speeds up to 100 m.p.h. But this is by no means the end of the story, for Britain's rail engineers and scientists are designing and building new trains to run at much higher speeds.

At present there are two; one of more usual design, the High Speed Train (H.S.T.) designed to run at 125 m.p.h., which is generally accepted as being about the fastest speed possible on existing type bogies* without causing discomfort to passengers, and another called the Advanced Passenger Train (A.P.T.) designed to run at 155 m.p.h.

The 'speed secret' of the A.P.T. lies in its revolutionary new self-steering bogies which were developed after years of study by British Rail's team of scientists at the Railway Technical Centre, Derby, birthplace of A.P.T. The sleek aerodynamic lines of an experimental A.P.T. are shown opposite. To increase passenger comfort on curves at high speed, the A.P.T.'s coaches tilt inwards creating the same stable conditions for passengers as does an aeroplane when it banks to change course, or a cyclist taking a corner.

With these exciting new trains, the day has now come when the mighty locomotive No. 71000 is as obsolete as 'Puffing Billy'. Yet the steam engine will always be honoured as a much loved part of the long history of railways in Britain, from the Stockton and Darlington Railway Company to British Railways.

*The wheels on main-line locomotives are secured in bogies. The Ladybird book 'How it works—The Locomotive' gives full details.

An artist's impression of the Advanced Passenger Train at speed